Make Money from the Comfort of Your Home

Guide on Effective Telecommuting While Taking Care of Your Family

By: Steven Campbell

9781635019926

I0510866

PUBLISHERS NOTES

Disclaimer – Speedy Publishing LLC

Speedy Publishing LLC

40 E Main Street, Newark, Delaware, 19711

Contact Us: 1-888-248-4521

Website: http://www.speedypublishing.co

REPRINTED Paperback Edition: 9781635019926:

Manufactured in the United States of America

DEDICATION

This book is dedicated to my wife, Michelle. Your unceasing love and loyalty to our family is extremely admirable.

TABLE OF CONTENTS

Chapter 1- The Joys of Working from Home

Lunch with friends, frequent coffee breaks and easy living are things that come up only when you are working from home. It's just like a dream come true for a person who wanted to enjoy life completely. Having a cup of coffee from your own coffee maker simply boasts your energy levels.

Work at home many advantages but it has a simple rule that states that no work then no money. Working at home doesn't mean that you have to enjoy your time only but you have to work also if you want to earn some money at the end.

You have to put some extra efforts in you work so that you can establish yourself as an expert. Working from home is exciting and yes it's true that you may get lazy or flexible but if you don't work hard or market your skills then it would be very difficult for you to get stability in your life.

Make Money from the Comfort of Your Home
When you wanted to take a holiday you can easily do that, if you wanted to set a higher salary level then you can also achieve that but the key is only the hard work and a desire to be a successful person in your field.

The ability to generate income while working at home is very exciting and attractive as well.

Many people are giving their resignations to their set office jobs just because they are attracted towards job at home. The luxurious and flexible life is simply attracting them.

There are number of reasons which make working at home more attractive. These reasons are simply arousing the urges of human being to enjoy their lives completely.

• While working at home, you can easily setup your schedule and can perform your tasks as per your mode

• You can easily eliminate your overhead expenses and increase your income levels

• The flexibility level that you enjoy while working at home is un-comparable.

• Working at home always give you a feeling of freedom which everyone wanted to enjoy

Paying daily expenses, meeting with deadlines, taxes and other issues are forcing individuals to go for work at home as by doing so all these would be eliminated dramatically. People are creating several ideas so that they can work at home and can get rid of many daily life problems. So, people are finding optimal solutions to generate income by different means while working at home at their regular 9 to 5 timings.

These reasons have enough weight to convince someone for looking into the matter. Along with this, the flexibility of lifestyle that one enjoys and income level that can be drawn by your own self are simply pulling individuals to have a serious consideration about this option.

The income that is earned from working at home can easily be comparable with any corporate sector salary. As the income is based upon the skills and personal abilities of the individuals due to which one can earn as much as he wanted to.

Normally, to get a big raise in your income either you have to start your own business or you may have to make a cut upon your monthly expenses.

Saving money for people who are working at home is much easier as compared to other people. They are used too of working in economic conditions so they can easily save money in any kind of circumstances.

To fulfill your dreams and to achieve your goals, working at home is the best way to go with. Normally an ambitious individual chooses this option so that high career objectives can be achieved.

The only thing is that you have to choose the right business as per your capabilities. After selection of business, simply market your abilities and earn a handsome amount of income for years and years.

Famous People and Businesses That Started from Home

There are number of world famous entrepreneurs who started their practical life with home business and now having a successful life.

Working at hope doesn't confirm your success but it offers you a peace of mind that allows you think and concentrate on your business completely. You can only fulfill your dreams when you can concentrate completely upon your work.

The Famous Sister Schubert

The famous lady used her kitchen to produce buttery rolls and blueberry breads. All these things were produced in her kitchen and then tested there as well.

The rolls from which she got fame are known as Everlasting Rolls and the recipe of these rolls was taken from family. She started her journey with catering business that was named as The Silver Spoon. This business was totally operated by her from her house.

She started all this from her kitchen and now she has her own manufacturing unit due to the huge business volume.

Microsoft Corporation

You have definitely heard about Microsoft or about Windows that is used in computers. All these things are developed by Microsoft who is owned by Bill gates.

Two young boys started a business of programming in a garage. At that stage they were at college and they started to do at their own. The achievement that is earned by him is simply awesome but the base of that achievement is working at home by exposing your abilities.

One can motivate itself by looking at the stories of these people. There are number of other great examples that are available in history. You can learn from them that how people started their practical life at their own and then attain the heights of success.

Chapter 2- Why Would You Want to Work From Home?

Working at home has many advantages as only an individual can explain the feelings that how good to feel being owner of your own self. For some people the advantages are known but to convince the remaining we have to pursue them.

If a person is working in a corporate sector or working in a manufacturing environment then it is enough for him to consider working at home to get a high level of income and without having any kind of restrictions as well.

Normally, in offices the environment is not flexible and limits the actions of the individuals. Every person is attracted towards flexibility and freedom in his job due to which working at home attracts the individuals very easily.

Day-to-Day Savings Mean Big

While working at home, you can save your day to day expenses like gas consumption etc. which ultimately give a rise to your income.

The vehicle you are using matters a lot in the gas consumption issue and distance of office from your house has a significant impact upon you gas charges.

According to a study, an average employee almost spends 1 to 3 hours per day in travelling from house to office. This means that an individual spends 15 hours per week only in travelling.

People spend hundreds of dollars on gas while travelling for their work. If you combine this average with the average of working hours per week that is of 40 hours then you will analyze that these hours are crossing the 50 mark.

These numbers are enough significant for any individual to consider the option of working at home.

Working at home not only reduces your stress levels that you have to absorb due to traffic but also reduces your travelling time and expenses as well.

Another factor that influence upon the decision of the individuals is that they have to make a proposal from their home computer and send it to the client. If accepted then they can start work from their home otherwise they can try another one.

Make Money from the Comfort of Your Home

You can easily avoid wear n tear expenses of your vehicle if you started to work at your home. Along with time, your gas expenses will also reduce by a significant amount. Regular maintenance expense will also cut down as the usage of vehicle reduces significantly.

It will put a direct impact on household budget as when you started to save your hundreds of dollars then they can be added in your household budget. By doing so, you can easily meet with your monthly expenses.

An additional thing that, if you started to work at your home then you don't have to worry about the gas prices which are fluctuating every now and then.

Still a Hands-On Parent

You can easily reduce your expense in terms of childcare and can give proper time to your children as well. You can enjoy your valuable moments with your family and can spend time of your own choice with them.

If you are doing a business that is not being disturbed with the presence of children or other family members then working at home is the right option to go with. You don't require any special concentration then you can give some time to your family and can share memorable moments with them.

It will be easy for you to attend several parent-teacher meetings at the school of your children. You can even enjoy the firsts of your children which is normally being missed by majority of men due to their job.

And the flexibility issue that comes again and again and the reason behind is its importance. One can enjoy the flexibility of his own managed schedule and can enjoy his work.

Many people wanted their own business to have self-satisfaction and belief due to which they choose work at home option. Parents aren't the only people who enjoy this deal but there are several other people who adopted this option for their own satisfaction.

If you want to work in a pajama at your bed in the middle of night then it can only happen if you are working at home. The casual style can only be adopted where you are the only one to control. Freedom of lifestyle is one of the big reasons due to which people switched to work at home deal.

Lovin' Flexibility

It is a dream for majority of people to manage their work and time as per their own choice. By moving towards right direction and having a proper planning one can easily make his dream true.

Flexibility simply allows you to manage not only your own responsibilities but also allows you to manage your family's responsibility too. You can easily amend your schedule if required to fulfill any other task of your family.

There are some important things for your family that you can't miss at any cost

You can easily reschedule your tasks if your child get sick then you can pick him/her from school and bring back to house.

Make Money from the Comfort of Your Home

If there are vacations then you don't have to give an application to get approved so that you can leave with your kids and if your application gets rejected then you can't do anything more.

It's very easy to handle these kinds of situations if you are working at home. You can plan your schedule as per the events and can windup your tasks well before time.

No Nice Clothes? No Worries!

One of the main advantages of working at home is that you don't have to worry about your clothes and accessories at all. In corporate sector it is an important thing to consider but while working at home you don't have to bother about these things. By doing so, your clothing expenses will also cut down with a significant amount.

Maintaining a wardrobe is not an easy task and one has to spend lots of money on this task. While working at home one doesn't have to keep update your wardrobe on regular basis. The simplest thing is that you can even work in your night dress at your home.

No More Germs from Other People

When you will work with different people then there might be chances of getting germs which will ultimately lead you towards illness. Working at home wouldn't only preserve you from illness but also reduces the chances of those working days that are missed due to illness.

However, you can't completely get rid from every kind of germs but you can simply save yourself from maximum exposure. This can only happen when you work at home instead of going to office.

Home-Cooked Meals

When you do a job in office then definitely all your meals will be from market or from a place like this. Sometimes, people have a restaurant near their office so they prefer to go to that restaurant due to shortage of time. In this case quality of food doesn't make much impact on decision making. As it is reported in a survey that $5 to $7 spends by people who work in corporate offices. On the yearly basis, this amount becomes $1,750 which is a huge one to spend.

In a corporate office, five to eight people do have their meals from outside. On the other hand, if you are working at home then you can easily access the food. You got penalty of options to choose from as your meal.

By having meals at home, you can't only save huge amount of money but can get nutritious food as well.

Exercise Like Planned

If you are working at home then you can easily schedule an exercise plan for yourself. If you wanted to go to a gym at the middle of the day then you can easily enjoy and manage your schedule in case of working at home. The flexibility that you get while working at home is simply incomparable with any other.

Normally, health and exercise are first priorities for any human being and as you can easily manage both these priorities so working at home is the best option to go with.

It is almost impossible that someone have to face any kind of disadvantage of working at home. The spark that is offered by working at home lifestyle can't be ignored by any human being. But one can easily justify that there is no major disadvantage of this kind of lifestyle.

CHAPTER 3- HOW TO COUNTER THE CONS OF WORKING FROM HOME

Like all other wonderful and exciting things, working at home also has some aspects that should be considered before finalizing it as your way.

All its disadvantages are related to the lifestyle of a person who is working at home. Except that this issue doesn't have any kind of disadvantage.

First of all you have to prepare yourself for starting such kind of business. You have to analyze yourself that are you ready for taking such kind of step? You have to look at some important aspects so that it would be easy to decide that either you have to take this step or not?

Patience Pays Off

You have to analyze that either you have sufficient patience to bear all the ups and downs of this business as it will take a long time to settle your business completely.

Either you have enough income to support yourself and to your family until your home based business started to generate income?

You have to consider the time that your business will take to generate decent income so that you can easily generate profits.

It totally depends upon your area of expertise and abilities that how long you can sustain in the market. You have to decide your final destination in order to successfully achieve it in your practical life.

You have to accurately analyze about your expenses so that you can have a figure of income that you have to earn at any cost for living your life. If your business can't give you the income which you required then it's useless to start such kind of business.

You have to judge that how much wait you have to do in order to attain satisfactory income levels? These are some realities that should be analyzed before the commencement of business so that you can keep patience up to that time limit.

You have to keep yourself steady so that you can easily pass these ups and downs of your business. Once you pass these starting ups and downs then you would start to earn a steady regular income.

When a person is used to of taking a fixed amount of check from the business then it's very hard for such people to adjust in such kind of jobs where there is uncertainty in the income.

Take Care of Your Own Benefits

When you have a family then job benefit becomes one of the major factors which can put a major influence upon your decision. Sometimes you need these befits to support your family and by doing so you can save hundreds of dollars.

Normally, these benefits possess health and life insurance, paid sick leaves, hospital expenses and etc. You should analyze both situations that if you have these benefits and if you don't have these benefits. In this way, you can easily analyze yourself and can have a clear picture of your future.

Nowadays, companies hire freelancers or people on contract so that they don't have to pay these benefits. So, you have to consider every possible situation. If you have to provide every benefit at your own then either you can provide these benefits to your family or not?

Time Management is a Must

When you are in decision making process then you have to give impedance to time allocation as well. You have to consider the amount of time that you have to give to your business so that your business can stabilize.

Although, there is much flexibility while working at home but till then you have to sacrifice some amount of time for your business. However, you are going to adopt the lifestyle of home based job so you have to give time to your job on this criterion as well.

If there is a deadline in your work then you have to meet that deadline at any cost. Either that time is of mid night or of after noon. It is obvious that meeting deadlines is the most important

Make Money from the Comfort of Your Home

thing in case of home base work. It's up to you that how you meet deadlines and manage all other activities that surrounds around you.

Properly utilization of time depends upon individuals. It's an ability that everyone has to implement by using his best talent. Time is one of those entities upon which no one has control. The only way to tackle time is to use best planning for time management else you can't do with this element of life.

Lifestyle of working at home is not every person. You have to consider and analyze the advantages and disadvantages of this lifestyle. Then you have to realize that either you can adjust in this lifestyle easily or not? If you realize that it's best for you then you have to proceed else just go with your current lifestyle.

How to Setup a Working Entrepreneurial System

When you started working at your home then actually you are going to start a new journey. This journey is full of fun, excitement emotions and ups and downs. You will experience different kinds of things and realize different experiences at different levels of business.

To make your business more rewarding, there are certain things that you have to perform so that you can achieve a successful career.

Ready Your Resume

A well written and good scripted resume always ensures you that you will get your required task. It doesn't matter that which kind of work you are doing or what work you are doing but your resume should be ready as it is being required by client at any time. If your resume is well written then you will definitely get the attention of other people.

You skills should be updates as per the requirements of the job and references are also being updated on regular basis.

As soon as you get a new skill or you get some specialization in an old skill then instantly put them on your resume.

You have to polish your resume as you are going to submit it in your corporate sector job. This is the best thing to follow so that you will definitely get attention of your client. A well prepared resume always put a great impact upon the person who wanted to hire your services.

You have to list all your job related experience along with your skill while sketching your resume. It's the most important aspect of resume so it should be handled with special attention.

You have to present yourself as persuasive so that you can convince the next person that you are the only right person for the job.

If you are applying for a data entry job then you have to convince the next person that how efficient you are in data working.

If you are applying for a marketing job then you have to present yourself in such a way that next person get convinced that you are the exact person to market their product.

Any kind of experience in eth field would present you as a polished professional which helps you in getting next job easily.

You should always present yourself as professional who has positive attitude because you have to attract your clients and this is the best way to go with.

There might be chances that your employer verifies your quoted references to have verification about you. The reference that you quoted in your resume should be updated and confirmed by yourself too.

You should have permission of using the references and the contact information of each reference should be correct.

Nowadays, resumes are communicated through emails so preparing a resume is as easy as typing some words in a word file. Online portals and e-mail are major sources of communicating resume to your desired place.

Dates and related description should be written correctly. You should check your resume for spelling mistakes along with grammatical errors so that you resume can be delivered error free.

To know about resume template and their structural flow, you can check already provided samples of resume within word file and can easily sketch a professional resume for yourself.

To gain the attention of the next person, you have to design your resume professionally and in this regard you can seek help from resume help services as well.

You can hire these services and can get better results as compared to other competitors. The prices of these services vary from person to person but you can set off this expense by the gain that you will gain from that job.

As resume is not going to be changed frequently so only you have to do is to just select a design and then provide your information.

Where's Your Productive Nook at Home?

When you make a decision about yourself that you are going to start working at your home then the next hurdle that will come across is that from when you would start working for your home based job.

You have to determine a clam and quite place for yourself as you have to spend a lot of time in front of computer. In this regard, you need some clam atmosphere so that you can concentrate on your proposals.

If you have lengthy working days at certain situations then your workplace should be capable of providing you such atmosphere that you can concentrate upon your job and can make correct decisions at that time.

Dedicated Email

If you are going to start a work base job then you should create an email id that is going to be used only for business purposes but that email id should be professional. No crazy or such kinds of words are involved in professional email ids.

In this way, you can easily keep your professional emails to one place and can easily track them too.

Schedule Your Working Hours

You have to setup your working schedule in advance and have to make sure that there would be no idle hours. While working, you should be at your best so that you can completely pay focus upon your work. You should avoid from extracurricular activities while your scheduled job time.

If you can't manage your time then it will be very harmful for your future and in such kind of cases people mostly got short of time while meeting deadlines. The flexibility that is the attractive point of working at home eventually takes you towards your downfall.

Update All Computer Applications When Needed

You have to keep your computer applications up to date as it will be very helpful for you in your future. If you keep your applications updates then you can keep yourself away from different kinds of viruses and Trojans easily.

You are required to run system scans after regular intervals of time. The efficiency and effectiveness increases by a significant margin. To attain the optimal productivity level, it is compulsory that you should possess latest applications on your computer.

If you don't want to lose your data then you have to take back up of all your important files at least once a week so that you can easily retrieve your data in case of any incident.

You should have latest and most secured antivirus system installed on your computer. Nowadays, computer viruses are so harmful that they almost completely destroy your data along with some hardware components.

CHAPTER 4- HOW TO AVOID ONLINE EMPLOYMENT SCAMS

As you are going to start work at home so you will be the easiest target for such kind of sites. These sites try to convince the people in their scam schemes and simply ditch them in just seconds of time. Most of these sites seem bogus when you simply enter into them. Their first look is telling everything about them.

You have to do lot of research work when you decided that you are going to start working at home. By doing this tiring work you only securing yourself and nothing more than that.

You have to keep a difference between legal and illegal work. As some of these sites are very convincing and attractive that no one can deny that offer so you have to open your sharp eye at every moment of time. When any offer come, you simply analyze the whole offer, their site and similar sort of things by your intelligence.

Make Money from the Comfort of Your Home

Some companies offer you easy earnings but they are very limited so you have to be very careful while choosing any of these options. You have to avoid from any kind of cost while starting job. When you visit these kinds of sites, most of them will be offering you easy earnings or offering you to be a millionaire in few days or like that. These are fake jobs and you have to do nothing with them.

These sites simply offer you wealth that can never be yours in reality. These kinds of scams are very tough to detect and realize. You should have an attentive mind so that you can easily pick them at early stages.

Here some points that will help you in detecting a scam or fake offer

- They will promise you that you will be rich in a very short span of time. You will start earning thousands of dollars at least with in that short time period.

- They would offer you that you don't have to do any kind of work to earn these catchy amounts. In reality, such kinds of income can never be legal where you are not required to put any kind of effort.

- Their address always is a P.O. Box number and it even can't be searched in Google as well. They will never provide you a real business address of their company.

- If you want to make a contact then you even can't do that because they only have form query option or an email address. Except that they have nothing in real to show.

These kinds of companies always target such kind of people who badly need a job or those who are very eager to earn money.

Desperation of such kind of people allows those scam people to trap them easily.

To sell their products or pack of services, they simply target such kind of people with emotions so that they can easily complete their task.

You can detect these kinds of scams by simply learning that what to look in a site and what kind of questions you have to ask from a site before started working. By doing so, you can easily save yourself from any kind of severe disaster. If you learn this technique then you can safely enjoy the ownership of your home based job.

So what you have to do in order to identify these scams and get rid them as well?

It's very simple as you have to remain away from such kind of sites which are offering membership fee to see the project details which they have.

They may be charging you fee for such kind of information that is readily available on the internet.

They try to hit you emotionally by figuring out your thinking, your mental approach and your financial condition by talking to you. Your conversation speaks a lot about your mental state. These sites started to be very aggressive upon you and dominate you in order to prove them superior and true. If once they do that then you will be a pie cake for them.

Most of the times, they trap you by providing fake information about their previous projects so that you will keep your interest in them and will try to get further information about them. Their main aim is to convince regardless of the fact that whatever way they have to adopt in this process.

The information that is provided by these sites is mostly paid and obviously fake as well. These stories are scripted in such a brilliant way that at first look no one can identify them that they are spam.

Look for a Reliable Work from Home Website

You are searching for work home site, and have opened one site and you see those beautiful and appealing views, expensive cars, exclusive village, big pools, nice hotels, superb foods and expensive clothing. These are just few of the many good things scammer sites can offer because they knew people are easily get carried with these luxuries to their advantage.

They will show you scripted testimonials from people that from nothing are now millionaires in just a matter of one month or even a week! I have had my share when I purchased a system for work at home for $49.99 and I tell you I almost freak out because it did not work out and what is bad about these opportunists is that, they target those who are really in need and broke like those who are unemployed, students, jobless moms. They target ones emotions of becoming free from debts and those big amount is really captivating.

The average person wants only little things to make life easier, these too good to be true offers are like a dream that they are persuaded to believe it can happen. Those big amounts of wealth are the things scammers are promising them. The presentations were so good that you will be encouraged to join today.

Be Wary of Where You Give Your Card Information To

These enormous claims of financial freedom make every one believe that it is the ultimate solution to their financial problem that they do not want to waste time and they act now! The offer is very irresistible that you cannot afford to lose it so you act immediately; you give your credit card number or your bank account number or even send money through western union. Guys do not do this!

Should You Believe in the Big Promises of Instant Cash?

Those big promises of instant cash, a week of tremendous wealth with no or little work at all are completely not true! Just imagine it, how can you get wealthy in an instant with small investment? Not even the wealthiest person will give away 1 million dollar for nothing; otherwise no one will work very hard if all these are true. Absolutely these are just one way of enticing you. Those advertisements are false!

One thing that you should take a look if the site is false or not is to meticulously examine the print at the end or base of the web site page; there you will see a very tiny message that is definitely made tiny print for a cause because they do not want you to know about it.

One thing is to read about the disclaimer. It says that, this site is not a guarantee, or this site is not an affiliate of or not registered of. This is the whole truth about the program. It will not guarantee you to earn that big money they are promising in the advertisement. A very clever scam site also comes in a stop watch on their site. And the phrase says there; make a decision now before time runs out! And another thing it say '30 people needed to complete and the system will be closed'. As an individual who doesn't want to miss the opportunity will be lured by joining and eventually paying.

Those are just strategies of these scammers who want to get money from you. If you are not carefully observing their tactics, you will be easily getting carried away because they trigger on your emotions. It only means one thing, they are encouraging you to buy by using your emotions before the product real identity is laid on you and before you realize it, and your money is gone. Those strategies are so clever that they focus on your emotions and probably your weakness.

Since they can get considerable amount of money from you they are not really concerned if that was your last dollar or what the system or program will do to your advantage. It's all to their advantage. If entertain and get carried by their advertisement, you soon regret it later after joining.

The truth it, those advertisement that says 30 members left to join or you have 24 hours to join before finally closing the system will literally be there and available even after a month of your joining. If you do not believe me, leave the site that says you only have 24 hours to join, after two days you come back and it is still there.

In other words, you have to properly scrutinize what you are joining into by effectively checking the promises, the claims and the benefits that these sites are offering you before you act and join now. Furthermore, be aware and guard yourself of the many scammers in the internet. this can be done by not rushing into your decision and not getting emotionally to their promises, but by evaluating the website, the business it offer and the reason why the product or services is being offered.

You have to evaluate on the following:

- Search for a genuine business

- Are they offering a reasonable price compared to the product they are offering?

- Will they require you to have down line, is it net working?

More often than not, the business idea has no significant to what they are offering and definitely there is no significant why you should take an immediate action or rush joining or it cannot give you large amount of money that will make a reason why someone like you and me will get in a hurry before they are gone.

Take time to know more about that company. The internet is your best resource in taking information for many companies with fifty, fifty credibility. Just type the company name on the internet search box or in Google, wherever you want to search them then you will see lots of comments, be thankful if it is good comments but most probably you will see bad comments.

Another thing that you should do to get reliable fact is to join forum so that you will know what members are saying to that company. There you will see various complaints from members who have joined the company offering.

You have to take note of the following:

- Did you see any complains about the company's services?

- Is the business a registered one?

- Did you find any customers who are satisfied with the product?

Make Money from the Comfort of Your Home

Accordingly, when you joined those home job opportunities, what did you really get that eventually change your perception about life and did that really made you rich? Basically all that you will get is a reading material that has general information on how to get wealthy, and generally they are very common advice from day today lives. Or it could be embarrassing sometimes when you see no information at all but just another site that will lets you join and again you have to pay for membership.

I will tell you this, you cannot find anything new in there, and they are all the same scam ideas wanting to get your money! Remember these scammers are geniuses trying to make new tricks to make you believe that it is something different when in fact it is just the same program and was repacked to lure you.

One thing that' you will get for sure is frustration and regret why you have joined such a scratch company. And another thing that is really sure to happen is that, these companies because they already have your information, like email address, will from time to time send you an email regarding the same or worst your credit card will be automatically debited every month.

Although it is quite improper to say but the only thing that these scammers can profit financially is to let someone (you and me) join and registered their company and pay. Once you are being recruited, you need to pay certain amount for membership and that payment will be chopped as commissions from your referrer and to the owner.

The bad part is that, it is hard to convince people to sign up or join, which is supposed to be you will get commission from them. The program is not and will never be the solution to your financial crisis in fact it will only put you into more debt.

These scammers will do everything to boost the program in any way he can. He would simply try to compensate from his effort and try to bring back the lost money. Sometimes they would say that there are faults on the recipient following to guidelines, which often result of not claiming the money.

Those excuses made by home business scams are attempted to redirect the fault and responsibility to the poor income seeker by placing all the blame on them and their lack of understanding. If you have only read those tiny prints located at the bottom of the page, you will see that they are dissolving any responsibility and legal action that a genuine company should take responsibility at. This action will exclude them of fiscal fund and the responsibility that lies on it.

It is very essential to follow advice, read that tiny message located at the last page of a web site, read a lot of information regarding the site and do not push through if the offer doesn't seem right. Paying for membership for a certain product that is too good to be true is absolutely a scam.

Scammers will do everything to make their ads appear like a legitimate one. Often times they place their program on job sites so that you won't hesitate to join them. They will make many strategies just to let you sold out with their program and eventually exposing them your account number.

You have to be careful with those promising jobs either, read at their ads, because it says there that they don't offer job but rather they provide you the job opening on another database. To keep away from sites like this, take note and record all the job sites you come across with. Record the site, the company, date you have applied and the website of if there is any information that will be beneficial as reference later.

Make Money from the Comfort of Your Home

This advice will save you from future regret and possible trouble as time goes on. It is alright to spend more time searching on the web for some useful information 'bout the company than regret later. This will also help you for easier access of the company whenever you need to contact them and most especially it will help you find an answer in the future when the company calls your attention.

I do not tell you not to apply for home job, but rather I encouraged you to apply all possible home jobs you may encounter but just beware of scams. Keep your credential updated, the more up to date your resume is, the more chances of getting hired. Most often than not, companies online will reply your application in a couple of months so do not get discouraged when it is almost a month and they did not contact you.

To narrow your search, type a specific job that applies to your ability and experience. Always take time to apply for several companies that offer same or relevant position to what you are applying for, this way you will not think of one company only but you have many options.

CHAPTER 5- HOW TO PROPERLY EXAMINE EVERY JOB OFFER

The work home community is an absolute place for scammers to breed and other opportunists. There are too many false offers and home base business in this kind of sites. There are those who do not collect money and there are those also who take a little amount of money from you. It is really hard to distinguish genuine and scam work home opportunity. But did you ever think why these jobs are enormous? Because mostly they are not legitimate businesses, though there are some that are legitimate.

But be aware also of those legitimate businesses since they are the target of these scammers. Scammers, because of their excellent knowledge of the internet, they can create a website that looks very similar to the legitimate site and there they will start their evil work. It needs a lot of time finding the legitimate one.

The most visible and obvious scam is when someone calls you or email you about a job offer that you never applied for or when you receive a mail informing you that you won lotto without even joining the site or worst without even placing a bet to them.

These sites come from unknown sites and the offer can never be trusted.

Learn the Modus Operandi of Scammers

These scammers use home job sites and take some information to possible victim, taking your complete name, email address, telephone number, and some vital information about you and from there they will have the chance to contact you and start digging more about you until you come to trust them. Your information is taken from forums database, or in jobs online on people who are searching for jobs. They are positive that people like you is easy to lure with because they are the people that needs money and immediate income and they pretense that they are the legitimate source of the job you are applying for.

The moment this scammers got your mail address, then they will work on that false job to make you believe that they are legitimate, and they will make everything so that they will get your trust and finally convince you to provide them your account number and credit card. If you happen to receive a mail like this, all you have to do is to delete them immediately without reading them.

Responding to their mail is of no use and will only put you into trouble because this email is only a test to check if the information they get is valid or not. If they verify that the information is valid, they will provide more and more job openings. Jobs that you can never resist its offer; if you delete them and do not response to their mail they will not also dare to mail you because they will think that the email is invalid or inactive.

One thing that is also not good is some legit companies are selling information of their members for money. Another designation of a scam site is that, they post jobs per hour on a certain site even when no company is offering a certain job. They will promise you a better job and a promising income, but they require something, it could be a payment from you.

If ever you encounter a job offer like this; a company that take information from you like bank account, credit card or ask you to send money in place of the job offered, you can report them to crime complaint' center in the internet. Most of these scammers claim that they are registered with the FBI and the NWCC Center. If you care to report these kinds of sites to the crime center you will definitely help the internet jobs legal and safe from scammers.

Programs to Stay Away From

There are those home businesses that are scams you have to be wary of this also. These scammers appear to be harmless, but the truth is they are dangerous because they can use your information to some more dangerous situations.

• **Lottery**

May I ask you did you bet on lottery online or have you won lottery online? Maybe you have won lottery online without even placing a bet, especially that UK lottery where they claim to have drawn your email in electronic lottery. This is basically true when you try to respond to one of their email and from time to time you will receive email stating that you won lottery sweepstakes.

Believe me those bulk emails that comes into your in box are scams and you should not respond to them. If you respond the first thing that they will do is to get vital information from you and then your account and if they cannot they will ask you to deposit money which they say for charges.

The moment you entertain their mails, the more that they will pressure you to send the money so that they can process the transaction, which according to them is the winning prize. Do not believe on them. I was one their victim, after sending the money, which they say are charges, then they never gets back to me and there is no way where I can get the money back because they never responded to my mail and this could also happen to you once you entertain them.

And there is also one thing, if you try to send them the amount, they require you again to send another as payment for other charges and you could lose big amount of money if you listen to them and before you realize it they are gone.

Once you realize it, your money is gone and there is no way where you can recover your money. Because the truth is the company never existed and the person who contacted you is a swindler and you have been scammed.

• **The Money Transfer**

Another scam that you will receive in your in box, is you will be required to dispose billing information such as address because they will send you millions of dollars, but to be able to process the transaction, you have to shoulder demurral charges or interest from Banks or they will ask someone who claims to be a representative.

Or it could be that a large sum of money was found dormant from a Bank and that they need a foreign partner in order to transfer the amount and your only participation is that, you will pay the attorney and other legal charges they claim and the money will be transferred to your account. There are two things involved here, if they are true (which is very impossible), you will have entered into an illegal transaction and you could be put to jail when auditing comes, or this act is very immoral for a professional to enter into this kind of transaction.

They will ask you to wire transfer the money, which they are claiming to be charges incurred during the process or they will ask you to send them via western union. They will provide you with complete transaction on where will you send the money and whose name will be written if ever you send the money. And do you know what's annoying with them? They will pressure you to send the money as soon as possible like there is no tomorrow.

If you entertain them and agree to pay the amount, then things will soon change into something complicated. You then will be persuaded to transfer the money into their hand waiting for that promise of millions that will never happen. This will appear like an answer to all your financial needs that you have been praying all your life. The bad thing is you will not know it is fraud until you have completed the transaction.

When you see an initial amount on your account, it feels like really genuine. Then you begin to initiate sending the money to that unknown contact, but after a week the checked that was deposited to your account was faked and you mess everything because you are get charged of the bounce check liability. As a result, the bank will be chasing you because of the big amount of liability when you deposited a bounce check and you are in a total chaos.

Per banks and lending policy all losses (bounce check is considered as losses), is a responsibility of the account holder. Any issue regarding financial discrepancy will be taken against you. The bank will not sympathized on what have happened to you, they care about their business and they do not care about your ignorance. And the nightmare falls back if you cannot pay the charges, chances are the bank will file a criminal case against you.

Without realizing it, you were into a money laundering act and the penalty is quite grave. You were fooled into giving cash, but the most awful situation is that, you can never do anything about it.

MLM Systems Are Scams in Disguise

This kind of marketing system is considered as scam and if ever you say they aren't scam, the chance of becoming a scam is so high. The multi marketing or commonly known as MLM is a kind of home base business with a concept of pyramiding scheme.

Basically, you become a member or affiliated service or a product by using it to convince people that the product is good and genuine. While you are using the product, you will also recommend it to your family and friends and then they will be required to join or become affiliate to be able to use the product. The person who makes MLM will make large amount of money and so those first 5 affiliates but below that, boy! You are only making those people rich and you leaving behind and broke.

Before you finalize your decision to join this kind of affiliation, first are you have to investigate and see who is behind that marketing system. To have a specific research, just type the company name and the word scam for example 'speed mobile scam' then it will bring you into more sites that tackles about members or affiliate of the company. From there you will know if the site is genuine or scam.

There you will also find out if the company has another online business. If it does then you know now and do not entertain any email from any companies related to the owner of that scam site.

You can also find criminal charges that the company or the owner might be involved with.

Most of these multi-level marketing do not carry a specific product or services that are valuable. You have to think wisely before finalizing your thought of joining a MLM. You have to research the business name and gather much information so that you can decide wisely.

CHAPTER 6- INCREASE YOUR CHANCES OF GETTING HIRED BY PROPER BRANDING

When you think of "branding", what comes to mind?

T.V commercials where their logo or mascot are repeatedly splashed across the screen?

If so, you're right on track. But when it comes to building a brand online as a freelance writer, you don't often have the funds needed for a mass scale campaign designed to highlight your skills and saturate the marketplaces with advertisements of your services.

The Grassroots Approach

Begin on a community forum where countless marketers are looking for quality content. Yes, you know that you could provide them your services but since you don't have a reputation yet then how can you convince employers to hire you?

You have to think from the perspective of a potential buyer who doesn't know you. While YOU know that you are an experienced and capable writer, they don't.

The first thought would probably be to offer samples of your work but every other writer is already doing that and it was unlikely that these busy marketers and business people had time to sift through every sample offered by you and other freelancers.

How Other Successful WFM Employees Built Their Brands

Other successful virtual employees built their brands using the following tips:

1) Get Their Attention.

Instead of offering a sample of your writing, which may not satisfy the employer's preferred writing style and topic, offer them a free article on the topic of their choice. This way, you can show them that you are an experienced and diversified writer. It also was content that they were allowed to use however they wished.

2) Jump Start the "Building Block" Phase

People had nothing to lose by accepting your free offer, and by doing it you and a potential employer both benefited. They were given free content and in exchange, this ultimately pushed them into hiring you for additional projects.

Not because they felt obligated to you but because consciously, when someone gives you something you become far more loyal to them, right? That barrier of skepticism and mistrust often associated with hiring new freelancers starts to lift and people are far more likely to respond to your offers.

Now, you want to be careful offering free content so that you focus your energy on securing as many clients as possible rather than just 'freebie seekers' (and there are many of those).

To do this, you can state that instead of offering content to the first XXX people who respond, you are manually selecting who to work with. This way, you can quickly determine whether those who respond are established marketers who are known to hire freelancers, or if perhaps it's someone who isn't likely to even consider hiring you for future projects.

Start by offering only 10 custom articles. Once those had been accepted, (which generated 5 orders from 8 of those people), offer it again, in rounds. Doing so makes it easier to manage projects and to keep things organized and what it also will do, is keep your offer in front of as many people as possible.

You won't have to run offers like this for too long, either. It's likely that after a few days of offering free work, if your quality is up to par, you will land enough clients to jump-start your freelance career. It really doesn't take much time at all if you strategically choose who to offer free content to, and make sure it's written in the style or voice that they've requested.

When building your brand you always want to focus on quality, not just in the actual projects you create, but in the way you handle every transaction. You want to keep in contact with the people you are writing for, you want to meet deadlines (even on free offers), and you want to use your offers as the foundation for building your online brand.

You also want to start building a reputation for value and integrity.

Every post you make on marketplaces or open communities should be written as though you are speaking directly to clients. You want to be careful that you don't give off the wrong impression and you can do this by retaining consistency in both the work you are paid to do and in your public writing styles.

This is a common mistake seen in many new freelance writers. They aren't particular about their writing style unless they are being paid for it. They don't go the extra mile in satisfying clients, and they aren't careful to accept only as many projects as they can actually complete on time. It's easy to get carried away when clients are anxious to outsource their projects to you, but if you aren't realistic about the work you can do within a specific timeframe, you'll risk credibility and ultimately destroy any chance you had that the client will hire you again.

For many freelancers, our work comes from only a small segment of our client base who consistently hires us again and again. This means it's critical that you work towards establishing a long-term relationship with your client base and that you do everything you can to go above and beyond with every order.

If you participate on freelance forums, it's likely that anyone considering hiring you is going to browse through your past posts and threads to get a feel for your writing style, your personality and of course, previous feedback and comments posted about you.

You want to make sure that when these people do a search on you that the only thing they find is consistent quality - experienced - personable and professionalism.

Earn Cash and Still Live a Very Active Lifestyle

So here's what you need to do to get more done, make more money and still have time to live your life the way you deserve to.

#1: Quantity Control

No, that doesn't read "quality control', although that's important too. Right now, we're talking about 'QUANTITY" control.

You absolutely need to limit the number of open projects that you accept; regardless of how badly you may need the extra income. Getting projects done quickly while being able to spend more time focusing on the quality of these projects will pay off dividends in the end as your clients are impressed with your quick turnaround times.

It's also important to limit the number of projects that you accept simply so that you don't get overwhelmed.

There are countless writers with such incredible potential who ruin their reputations simply because they bit off far more than they could chew, resulting in projects being late, people complaining on public forums and marketplaces, and ultimately, requesting refunds or being difficult to please once they did receive their project because they had programmed their minds that because the content provider appeared unreliable that they wouldn't be happy with the content, regardless of the quality.

#2: Focus On JUST ONE Project at a Time

When you receive a project or are hired to create custom content, you want to create a queue and work on each individual project ONE at a time.

This doesn't mean you can't accept multiple projects at once, you can and you should. But if you start working on a number of projects at once, you will not only become confused (having to refresh your memory each time you go back to work on it), the quality will suffer.

Let clients know that their project will be completed by a specific date, and always allow yourself adequate time to complete the work.

You don't want to be overzealous in trying to impress clients with a quick delivery date and not be able to meet it. Instead, give them a delivery date that is realistic and do your best to always deliver a day ahead. It will do wonders for building client loyalty and generating repeat business.

#3: Create A MAINTAINABLE Schedule

You will want to adapt a schedule that works around your high and low points during the day.

If you find you are more productive writing earlier in the day, set your alarm an hour earlier to give you time to wake up and be alert. Or if you find that you write better late at night, perhaps

Make Money from the Comfort of Your Home
when the kids are asleep and the house is silent, work in a few extra hours to boost your overall productivity.

It takes work to adapt to a strict schedule and in many cases, especially if you are a stay at home parent; it just won't always be so easy to stick with a regular routine.

Just do your best to identify the times of day you are at your best and try to squeeze in some work time during that portion of your day.

ABOUT THE AUTHOR

Steven Campbell is a retired professor who now owns several online job search websites.

Steven was born in Alaska in a family of businessmen. It came as no surprise when he decided to take business management in college and soon taught at the local university. He was, however, the first member of the family to tap technology when it comes to maximizing profits.

Today, Steven's websites have helped pair over 12,000 virtual employees to their employers.